Learn Bitcoin Basics 2021
Easy-to-read guide to what Bitcoin is

Copyright © 2021

All rights reserved. No part of this book may be used or reproduced by any means, graphic, electronic, or mechanical, including photocopying, recording, taping, or by any information storage retrieval system, without the written permission of the publisher except in the case of brief quotations embodied in critical articles and reviews.

Table of Contents

Preface

Chapter 1: The who, and why it matters

Chapter 2: The when and the why – People power?

Chapter 3: What is Bitcoin – is it fish or fowl?

Chapter 4: How does it work? – The digital nuts and bolts

Chapter 5: How do I buy Bitcoin? – The deal is done

Chapter 6: What can I do with my Bitcoin? Do I spend it or save it?

Chapter 7: Is Bitcoin safe? – Where did my Bitcoin go?

Chapter 8: Bitcoin Pros and Cons

Preface

This book is not, and never was intended to be, an in-depth study of Bitcoin or its workings, or of blockchain, or indeed the history and workings of the financial system. It was always intended to be a relatively short and easy-to-read guide to what Bitcoin is.

It seems that you can hardly pick up a paper or look at a newsfeed without seeing a story about Bitcoin or some other cryptocurrency. You know the sort of stuff: "One Bitcoin will be worth the same as a new Lamborghini by the end of the year," or "Cryptocurrency is being used to finance all the gun-running and drug trade in the world." For most of us, the first question that pops into our heads is "What is this thing that seems so important to our lives?" So, as my starting point, I looked at the various search engines and cryptocurrency or Bitcoin forums to see what the most frequently asked questions were.

I have not attempted to answer questions such as "Which cryptocurrency will be worth the most this year?" or "Will Bitcoin be worth $100,000 next month?" First, I'm not a financial adviser. Second, even the most knowledgeable gurus with all their technical tools don't know these things with any certainty. The best they can do is offer an educated guess. There are too many variables and unknowns which could knock the market off a predicted course at any time.

As a result of my research, I decided to provide an overview of the basics about Bitcoin. Why and when it was created. What it is and how it works. How you obtain it and what you can do with it.

I trust that once you have finished reading this book you will have gained a basic understanding of Bitcoin – enough at least to understand what news reports mean. Perhaps you will be stirred to undertake further research to gain a better knowledge of Bitcoin. Your effort will be repaid. One way or another, Bitcoin is set to have big impact on all our lives.

Chapter 1

The who, and why it matters

The identity of the author of Bitcoin is still a mystery. Over recent years there have been claims and counter-claims to authorship, which have been vigorously litigated.

However, what is undeniable is that in 2008 Satoshi Nakamoto published a white paper which led to the development of cryptocurrency. This paper, called "Bitcoin: A Peer-to-Peer Electronic Cash System", described how the use of a peer-to-peer network could resolve the issue of double-spending within a digital currency. Bitcoin was born.

So, who is or was Satoshi Nakamoto? No single individual of that name, who has a valid claim to authorship, has been found. This has led to a consensus that the name is a pseudonym for one person or a group of persons who wish to remain anonymous. Nakamoto ended their involvement with Bitcoin in 2010, saying in an email that they had "moved on to other things". The mystery surrounding the identity of Nakamoto has led to considerable speculation as to who Nakamoto really is, especially given the growing visibility and popularity of cryptocurrencies.

Several people have been identified as, or have claimed to be, Satoshi Nakamoto. None so far has provided definitive proof that they are Nakamoto. These are some of the names put forward:

1. **Dorian Nakamoto**, a California-based academic and engineer. Apparently, based mainly on his surname, Mr Nakamoto was suggested as Bitcoin's creator by a Newsweek article in 2014. This was quickly denied by Dorian Nakamoto.

2. **Hal Finney**, a cryptographer, was also suggested. Finney was the first person to receive Bitcoins from Nakamoto. He also was very active in the field of cryptocurrency technology and exchanged several posts on Bitcoin discussion forums with Nakamoto. This has naturally led to debate regarding his

involvement in the creation of Bitcoin. Finney died in 2014.

3. **<u>Nick Szabo</u>** is another cryptographer who wrote a blog on a digital currency called Bit Gold in 2005. This project was very similar to Bitcoin, and has led some people to put him forward as Bitcoin's creator. This is despite the fact he does not seem to have had any direct involvement with Bitcoin itself.

4. **<u>Craig Wright</u>** is an Australian computer scientist, academic and businessman, who is probably the best-known claimant to the title of Nakamoto. Since 2015 Wright has been trying to prove, so far unsuccessfully, that with the help of "others" he is the creator of Bitcoin.

<u>In support of his claim, Wright:</u>

- has claimed that under the pseudonym Satoshi Nakamoto he completed the Bitcoin project started in 1997 and that it was filed with the Australian government.
- has claimed to be the main part of the team which created Bitcoin, in interviews with

The Economist, GQ and the BBC in 2016.

- successfully applied in 2019 to the US Copyright Registry to be registered as the author of the 2008 white paper. However, it turns out that anyone can register a claim to copyright in this way, and that other people have made the same claim to the white paper at the US Copyright Office.
- has instructed his lawyers to demand that the websites Bitcoin.org and Bitcoincore.org remove Satoshi Nakamoto's white paper from their platforms, alleging that they are violating copyright laws.
- is defending a court case brought by the brother of David Kleiman, whom Wright described in emails as his best friend and business partner. Kleiman died in 2013. His brother Ira is now

suing Wright on behalf of his brother's estate for up to half of the Bitcoin thought to be held in trusts. Wright has admitted in an email that "I had an idea, but it would never have been executed without Dave." The odd thing about this action is that Kleiman's whole case rests on the fact that Wright is Nakamoto and that he controls the Bitcoins, even though Wright has yet to establish either that he is Nakamoto or that he has control over the Bitcoins. The case is due to be heard in June 2021.

- with the help of a ruling of the Court of Appeal in London, is suing Magnus Granath, a Norwegian technology commentator, for defamation. Granath posted on Twitter that Wright was attempting to "fraudulently 'prove' he is Satoshi." He added: "Never forget. #CraigWrightIsAFraud." Wright's legal team said in court that he "has not fraudulently claimed to be Satoshi Nakamoto — he is Satoshi Nakamoto."

So whether Nakamoto is found to be Wright, or one of the other candidates, or indeed someone yet to feature in the speculation regarding his identity, is a modern day whodunnit. Some even argue that Nakamoto should remain anonymous. This view is based on the argument the only point of failure that Bitcoin could have is the person who created it. Once that individual is removed, there is no one person who can influence the direction Bitcoin takes. In Wright's case, we will have to wait for the outcome of the various court actions to see whether his claims are vindicated.

Why does it matter?

It is understandable, perhaps, to take the attitude "Why would it matter to me who created Bitcoin?" or even to think "If he wants to remain anonymous that's fine by me", or "Well, the courts will sort out whether or not Wright is Nakamoto."

But yes, it does matter. Here's why. Bitcoin, like it or not, has had an immense impact on the financial system and big business. You may have a pension, or have invested in stocks and shares, or bought into a fund that operates on the stock market or any of the other investment vehicles. If so, you undoubtedly have exposure to Bitcoin, either directly or indirectly.

How has that happened? Big institutions have enthusiastically bought into Bitcoin. Tesla has just bought 1.5 billion dollars' worth. It has been widely speculated in the financial press that Apple and Twitter may follow suit. Although J P Morgan say they are thinking of buying some Bitcoin only at the right time, they do have a large stake in MicroStrategy, which holds a significant amount of Bitcoin.

So again, why would that matter? Simply because Nakamoto holds 1.1 million Bitcoin, currently worth around $5.5 billion. That equates to around 5% of all available Bitcoin. If Nakamoto is dead, or his Bitcoins are lost, then there won't be any activity relating to them and Bitcoin's scarcity value will be maintained. However, if Nakamoto is found, then the picture changes considerably. In May 2020, a rumour started on Twitter that around $400,000 of Bitcoin had been transferred from a Bitcoin wallet owned by Nakamoto to another unknown Bitcoin wallet. Fears that Nakamoto was dumping his Bitcoin prompted an immediate wave of selling. Bitcoin's price immediately dropped by 4%. This happened even though all the reliable indicators showed that someone other than Nakamoto was responsible for the transaction. This demonstrates how volatile cryptocurrencies can be, and how, as big business gets involved with Bitcoin and other cryptocurrencies, that volatility could feed into mainstream stocks and shares prices. And that is how Nakamoto's identity and the fate of his Bitcoins could affect your pension or investments.

Chapter 2

The when and the why – People power?

As the when helps to answer the why, we can deal with these two issues together.

To understand the when and the why, we must take a brief look at the financial crash of 2007 and its consequences. From 2001, banks in the USA systematically reduced their interest rates to such an extent that people who normally wouldn't qualify for a loan were able to obtain mortgages. This became known as subprime lending. Naturally, this led to a huge increase in the demand for housing. House prices, obviously, rose as a result. This was fine until 2005, when interest rates started to go up. The demand for houses, even among the relatively well off, went down. House prices, of course, fell as a result.

This was where the wheels started to fall off the wagon. The subprime borrowers couldn't afford their mortgage repayments. As house prices fell, the usual routes out of this situation became unavailable. The borrowers could not sell their houses at a profit to pay off their mortgage, nor could they re-mortgage their house against the increased value of their home. As a result, increasing numbers of borrowers found that they owed more on their mortgage than their house was worth, and they defaulted on their loans. Faced with rising foreclosures, the banks stopped granting subprime mortgages. This led to a further drop in demand and a fall in house prices.

Inevitably, the subprime mortgage market collapsed. This led to many banks finding themselves in deep trouble. In the years up to 2007 the entire financial industry had heavily invested in increasingly speculative and risky derivatives, which were for the most part unregulated. When the crash came, the banks found to their horror that a significant part of their assets comprised subprime loans or derivatives, of dubious value, which came to be known as toxic assets.

Since the financial industry heavily invested in mortgage-backed derivatives, the housing industry's downturn became a calamity for the financial industry. The trust between banks broke down, as each began to doubt the others' solvency. This led to the almost unheard-of situation of banks refusing to lend to each other. As a result, there was an interbank credit freeze. Many banks and financial institutions, even well-known and respected names, were forced to seek government bailouts, merge with other institutions, or declare bankruptcy. The situation was so bad that, worldwide, 84 banks or financial institutions were affected. Of these, 10 were declared bankrupt, 31 were taken over either partially or wholly by national governments or governmental bodies, and the rest were acquired by other institutions.

This created a massive reduction in the availability of credit to even the most financially secure customers. Businesses who relied on consumer credit to sell their products were badly hit. Accordingly, businesses had to cut costs, business in general contracted, and employees were laid off. For example, in 2009 both General Motors and Chrysler declared bankruptcy and went into partial government ownership through a bailout program.

In the USA, between 2007 and 2009, GDP declined by 4.3%, unemployment rose between 4.5 and 5%, and the S&P 500 index fell by 57%. Most industrialised countries suffered economic slowdowns. Many banks in western Europe had invested in the same type of securities as the US banks and suffered the same fate. Spain, Greece, Ireland, Italy, and Portugal all suffered sovereign debt crises. The European Union, the European Central Bank and the IMF had to provide bailouts, which came with strict conditions. To meet these conditions, the recipient governments had to take austerity measures that were deeply unpopular and resented in their countries. In Iceland, the country's three largest banks had to be taken into government ownership; a particularly severe recession followed, and the government fell.

All this meant that an increasing number of people couldn't pay their mortgages, which only served to exacerbate the situation. The human cost was devastating. Millions of people lost their jobs and their homes, the divorce rate went up, and families were torn apart. A quarter of US households lost 75% of their net worth and more than 50% lost 25%. There was visceral anger at the havoc that had been wrought upon the world. People wanted someone to accept responsibility for this catastrophe and to be held accountable.

Out of this tragedy, confidence in governments, financial regulators, central bankers, and bankers in general, fell to an all-time low. There was widespread incomprehension at how this situation could have been allowed to occur. The blame was widely placed on:

- bankers, for what was perceived to be their greedy and self-serving drive to create, promote and sell increasingly speculative derivates to inflate their already substantial yearly bonuses.

- financial regulators, for appearing to have been asleep at the wheel while all this was going on, and for not enforcing existing regulations forcefully enough.

- central bankers, for ignoring warning signs of the looming crash and failing to do anything to stop it.

- governments, for allowing the banking industry to get away with "light touch" regulation and supervision that enabled banks to create a crisis which almost brought down the global financial system. The response of governments to the crash was also viewed with some scepticism. To reinvigorate their economies, governments embarked on a round of "quantitative easing." This entailed printing vast amounts of money, which for some raised the spectre of huge inflationary pressures and the debasement of their country's currency.

It was felt across the world that banks and governments were to blame for the mess. They had shown they could not be trusted to run the financial system, and that they had lost the right to do so.

It was against this backdrop that in February 2009, Nakamoto wrote on an online forum:

"The root problem with conventional currency is all the trust that's required to make it work. The central bank must be trusted not to debase the currency, but the history of fiat currencies is full of breaches of that trust. Banks must be trusted to hold our money and transfer it electronically, but they lend it out in waves of credit bubbles with barely a fraction in reserve."

So, what was Nakamoto's solution to this problem, and what did he hope to achieve? The reason he gave for creating Bitcoin was to provide an alternative to traditional money. He was going to provide a peer-to-peer digital payment system that did not need third-party confirmation by the banks or other financial institutions.

Under the existing system, the banks were required to be involved in every digital monetary transaction, whatever its size. In conducting these transactions the banks incurred costs, which they then passed on to end users. This meant that the banks, the credit card companies such as Visa and Mastercard, and similar institutions which controlled the electronic payment system, received a substantial income from the fees generated. For example, Visa made over $19 billion from fees in 2015. This alone was a great incentive to invent Bitcoin.

So, apart from dispensing with expensive third parties to a transaction, what did Nakamoto seek to achieve with Bitcoin, and what risks or abuses did he hope to end?

In his online post he specifically notes that "Banks must be trusted to hold our money …but they lend it out in waves of credit bubbles." What is he getting at here? Well, we put our money in banks to keep it secure and sometimes to receive interest on that money. The banks, in the ordinary course of their business, lend the money to others. They charge interest, which gives them a profit and funds their business activities, and where appropriate they pay interest to depositors. So far so good. This is good for society as a whole, as it means that people can borrow money to buy houses, cars and so on. Companies can borrow money to expand their businesses and hire more workers. Where it all starts to go wrong is when the banks get involved in complex financial instruments, such as derivatives, with multiple participants and lower levels of clarity regarding the nature of the security. This can lead to situations such as the crash of 2008, where huge losses are incurred through unsustainable levels of lending when there is a correction in the market.

Why do the banks get involved with this kind of security? The simple answer is that they are rewarded for doing so. There are great incentives to take big risks. Banks are paid large fees to have a lenient lending policy and to lend irrespective of the probity of their lending. Investment banks are paid fees for pooling risky loans into securities, which they sell to investors. In the early 2000s, investment banks sold derivatives to investors knowing that they were based on loans which were never likely to be repaid. When the crash came, governments had to bail out the financial institutions because they were "too big to fail".

This is just one example of how the present centralised financial system is systemically flawed. Financial institutions are paid well to provide risky loans to people who would not qualify under a more prudent lending regime. They do so in the full knowledge that if it all goes wrong, they will not have to bear the cost. The taxpayer will pick up the tab at the end of the day. Nakamoto, clearly saw this as a breach of the trust between the banks and their depositors. By creating Bitcoin, he provided a system where the need for banks to store your wealth is obviated. You can put Bitcoin in your digital wallet and look after it yourself. This stops banks using your money to make highly speculative and risky loans.

Nakamoto's online post also refers to the trust in central bankers to do nothing to "debase the currency." Have central banks repaid that trust? Central banks across the world used taxpayers' money to bail out financial institutions. They were also left with the task of trying to fix a broken financial system. To do this, they employed the type of monetary policy advocated by John Maynard Keynes. This encompasses, among other things, increased government spending to stimulate demand. The central banks also adjusted the lending rates between banks and the level of money each bank should hold as a reserve. "Quantitative easing", that is, printing more money, was also employed.

There is perhaps a good argument that without quantitative easing the 2008 crash could have been far worse. However, increasing the monetary supply may create inflationary pressures and debase the currency at the expense of the economy. There is also a temptation for governments to print more money to pay off their debts. Since 2016, despite strong opposition, the US government has raised the debt to GDP ratio to 106%, a record high. In fact, 75% of all US dollars in existence were printed after 2009.

By the way, a decentralised financial system is not a new idea. In 1892 the eminent Austrian economist Carl Menger wrote "Money is not an invention of the state. It is not the product of a legislative act. Even the sanction of political authority is not necessary for its existence. Certain commodities came to be money quite naturally, as the result of economic relationships that were independent of the power of the state". In 1976 the Austrian economist and Nobel prize-winner Friedrich Hayek denounced inflation as a major threat to private enterprise and the functioning of a free society. In his book Denationalization of Money, Hayek wrote "As soon as one succeeds in freeing oneself of the universally but tacitly accepted creed that a country must be supplied by its government with its own distinctive and exclusive currency, all sorts of interesting questions arise which have never been examined."

Out of the clear breach of trust by the bankers and governments came a desire for, and pressure to create, a decentralised financial system. The result was Bitcoin. Bitcoin is not issued by governments. The maximum amount of Bitcoin that can be in existence is pegged at 21 million. This can only be increased by a majority of the holders voting for such an increase. Furthermore, you do not need banks to store your Bitcoin. You can do that yourself. This, of course, means that the banks can no longer gamble with your money.

As though by way of explanation for Bitcoin's creation, you will find contained in its genesis block the following message: "The Times 03/Jan/2009 Chancellor on brink of second bailout for banks". This was the headline of The Times newspaper on the day that the block was generated.

Chapter 3

What is Bitcoin – is it fish or fowl?

If you look at any cryptocurrency forum you will see that the most popular questions are "What is Bitcoin and what does it do?" and "What is Bitcoin and how does it work?" The various answers to "What is Bitcoin" are in essence all the same, although the definitions may be couched in slightly different wording. Generally they deal only with what Bitcoin has "under the hood". This is OK, but is that really the sum total of what Bitcoin is? Doesn't the question encompass other questions such as:

- Is Bitcoin a currency?
- Is Bitcoin a commodity?
- Is Bitcoin a security?
- Is Bitcoin a bit of all three?
- Is Bitcoin a hedge against inflation?
- Is Bitcoin an alternative to gold?
- Is Bitcoin a scam?
- When you buy Bitcoin what do you get for your money?

So, to deal with the what's "under the hood" part of the question – "What is Bitcoin?" – let's go to Bitcoin.org. This is the website registered by Satoshi Nakamoto and his fellow developer Martii Malmi. If anyone should know what Bitcoin is, it should be them. This website defines Bitcoin as follows:

"Bitcoin uses peer-to-peer technology to operate with no central authority or banks; managing transactions and the issuing of Bitcoins is carried out collectively by the network. **Bitcoin is open source; its design is public, nobody owns or controls Bitcoin and everyone can take part.** Through many of its unique properties, Bitcoin allows exciting uses that could not be covered by any previous payment system."

So what does all that mean?

- Bitcoin is digital money; it does not have any physical form.

- You can keep it, buy goods and services with it, send it anywhere in the world, essentially do anything that you can do with traditional money. You can do this 24/7, securely and at very low cost. The key difference is that you don't need a bank's involvement to do any of this, meaning no expensive bank fees and delays due to the nature of the bank's systems or business hours.

- Its decentralised nature means no one owns Bitcoin. It can't be claimed by any individual or country and its usage can't be bent to the wishes of any individual or individual country.

- As it is a peer-to-peer system, only the sender and recipient are involved in any transaction. There isn't any requirement for anyone else to process the payment.

- All Bitcoin transactions are recorded, using Bitcoin, on an open public ledger. Anyone can see the ledger, but it is virtually impossible to tamper with it or shut it down.

Turning to the questions of whether Bitcoin is a currency, a security, a commodity or a combination of the three, let us look at definitions of these three entities. We may then be in a better position to answer these questions.

- **Currency.** In an Investopedia article, Jake Frankenfield defined currency as "a medium of exchange for goods and services. In short, it's money, in the form of paper or coins, usually issued by a government and generally accepted at its face value as a method of payment… A key characteristic of modern money is that it is uniformly worthless in itself. That is, bills are pieces of paper rather than coins made of gold, silver, or bronze."

- **Security.** In an Investopedia article, Will Kenton defined a security as "a fungible, negotiable financial instrument that holds some type of monetary value. It represents an ownership position in a publicly-traded corporation via stock; a creditor relationship with a governmental body or a corporation represented by owning that entity's bond; or rights to ownership as represented by an option."

- **Commodity.** In an Investopedia article, Jason Fernando defined a commodity as "a basic good used in commerce that is interchangeable with other goods of the same type. Commodities are most often used as inputs in the production of other goods or services. The quality of a given commodity may differ slightly, but it is essentially uniform across producers. When they are traded on an exchange, commodities must also meet specified minimum standards, also known as a basis grade. They tend to change rapidly from year to year."

Now let's look at Bitcoin in the light of these definitions. In terms of its being a currency, you can certainly buy and sell goods and services using Bitcoin. Craig Wright, the self-proclaimed inventor of Bitcoin, has said that Bitcoin "was meant to be a successor to cash not a tool of speculation." Famously, in one of the first Bitcoin transactions, Laszlo Hanyesz offered and paid 10,000 Bitcoins for two Papa John's pizzas. Since then, over 100,000 other outlets have decided to accept Bitcoin as payment. However, from here things get a bit more complicated and possibly confusing. One of the main purposes of a currency is to facilitate trade. Does Bitcoin actually achieve this? On the one hand, since 2018 Bitcoin seems to have moved away from its role as a currency, and its trading volumes have fallen. This may have several causes. First, there is the question of Bitcoin's volatility. For a currency to function properly it needs stability so that buyers and sellers know what value they will receive for their goods or services. If a trader agrees a price, but the transaction takes several days to complete, the price of Bitcoin may rise or fall. This could have a significant effect on whether the trader makes a profit or loss. Major currencies tend to have an annual volatility rate of between 0.5% and 1% every 30–60 days. However, Bitcoin's volatility rate has hovered between 4% and 5% in 2018, and more recently by 2.25% over 60 days. This could pose an obstacle to Bitcoin's ready acceptance as a currency. Another obstacle is the question of the rate of dealing with transactions. In an interview with Bloomberg Television, Professor Nouriel Roubini of New York University's Stern School of Business, said: "Fundamentally, Bitcoin is not a currency. The technology doesn't allow more than five transactions per second. The Visa network allows you 24,000. It's never going to be used for goods and services." Lastly, there can only be 21 million Bitcoins. This imposes limitations on the number of Bitcoins that are in circulation at any time. However, there is a growing trend for institutional investors to buy up Bitcoins and store them. In its "Valuing Bitcoin" report, Grayscale, the leading cryptocurrency asset manager, highlighted the increase in the number of people holding Bitcoin for longer than three years compared with the number of people who had traded Bitcoin within 90 days.

On the other hand, major companies are embracing Bitcoin as a currency. Visa has set out a road map to support Bitcoin. Mastercard has said it will enable more merchants to accept certain digital currencies in 2021. Digital payment companies such as PayPal and Square already allow Bitcoin on their platforms, and BNY Mellon, America's oldest bank, has said it will provide banking services for cryptocurrencies. Tesla has announced that it will accept Bitcoin as payment for its cars. Citibank analysts have suggested that Bitcoin could be "optimally positioned to become the preferred currency for global trade."

So history would seem to show that Bitcoin started out as a currency, that it went through a phase in which it was treated as something else, but that there is now new impetus to use it as a currency once more.

If Bitcoin isn't a currency is it a security? Well, to be a security Bitcoin must satisfy the definition of a security, that is, it must be a "fungible, negotiable financial instrument that holds some type of monetary value." Bitcoin does seem to pass this test, because it is fungible, it is a negotiable financial instrument, and it has monetary value. It also satisfies the ownership criteria. It has been said that Tesla made more money from Elon Musk's investment of $1.5 billion in Bitcoin than from manufacturing its cars. MicroStrategy made a return of $133 million on its $550 million investment in Bitcoin. Although Bitcoin may fit the definition, William Hinman of the SEC has said "Bitcoin is not a security". It should also be noted that government regulators in both the US and South Korea are treating Bitcoin as a type of commodity rather than as a security. At the same time, regulators in both the European Union and the UK seem more inclined to treat it as a currency.

So that just leaves the question of whether Bitcoin is a commodity. As a rule of thumb, a commodity has the same characteristics whoever produces it. Traditional commodities include:

- Grains
- Gold
- Beef
- Oil
- Natural Gas
- Foreign currencies

In the US, the Commodities Futures Trading Commission classified Bitcoin as a commodity in 2015.

So, what does this mean? Commodities generally tend to have greater price volatility than other assets. This makes them a favoured arena for speculators trying to predict price movement of these classes of assets. In 2017 the Chicago Board Options Exchange launched the first Bitcoin futures product. This now accounts for around 75% of all Bitcoin trade volume. A spokesperson from AAX, the world's first digital asset exchange powered by the London Stock Exchange, has said that "Bitcoin's volatility lends itself well to futures trading."

It is worth pointing out that Bitcoin is more regulated as a commodity than it is as a currency or as a security. The Chicago Board Options Exchange imposes regulations which may be used to remove non-compliant exchanges. Because investors are not required to hold the underlying asset in the futures market, institutional investors have shown particular interest. This has resulted in the view that Bitcoin is primarily a commodity.

So, what is Bitcoin and why does this matter? Well, when you buy Bitcoin you need to know whether it is a currency, an asset or a commodity. This is because its definition will determine how it is regulated.

We have seen that Bitcoin can be:

- a currency which can be used to buy and sell goods and services.
- an asset which can be used as an investment.
- a commodity which can be traded for similar products on the crypto markets.

So it would appear that in the final analysis, all three classifications are acceptable. What really determines what category Bitcoin falls in is how it is used by the holder. Really, Bitcoin is so versatile it is invidious to try to shoehorn it into a single classification.

We now turn to the question of whether Bitcoin is a hedge against inflation. We have seen that countries across the world have used quantitative easing to increase the money supply. This has created fears of inflationary pressures. Michael Saylor, the CEO of MicroStrategy, has pointed out that as central banks increase the supply of a currency, so the value of everything bought with that currency, including equities and bonds, becomes worth less. Bitcoin, by contrast, has a fixed monetary supply, which can't be changed and is non-inflationary. It is for that reason that it is seen as a hedge against inflation.

Is Bitcoin an alternative to gold? As we have seen, Bitcoin, like gold, may be treated as a commodity. Gold is not a particularly profitable investment under normal conditions. However, in times of market or global turbulence, when people are seeking a safe haven for their wealth, investors traditionally turn to gold. In recent times Bitcoin has seemed to some an alternative to gold. In gold's favour, when you buy it, you have something tangible. Whilst it is true that the price of gold can go up and down, it is nowhere near as volatile as Bitcoin. However, gold is expensive to transport and store, costs which do not affect Bitcoin. Mansoor Mohi-uddin, Chief Economist at the Bank of Singapore, has suggested that Bitcoin could replace traditional safe haven assets like gold. In his research note he pointed out that due to Bitcoin's finite supply, investors were increasingly looking to add it to their portfolios, although some concerns remained regarding its regulation and its rather chequered history. He described the prerequisites for Bitcoin to replace gold: "First, investors need trustworthy institutions to be able to hold digital currencies securely. Second, liquidity needs to improve significantly to reduce volatility to manageable levels." So as we have seen, Bitcoin can be an alternative to gold. It may well replace gold as the premier safe haven asset, but not just yet.

Is Bitcoin a scam? An interesting question. Craig Wright famously said "I invented Bitcoin – now it's a Ponzi scheme." Bill Harris, the former CEO of Intuit and a founding CEO of PayPal and Personal Capital has commented that "In my opinion, it's a colossal pump and dump scheme the likes of which the world has never seen. In a pump and dump game promotors 'pump' up the price of a security creating a speculative frenzy then 'dump' some of their holdings at artificially high prices. And some cryptocurrencies are pure frauds. Ernst & Young estimates that 10 per cent of the money raised for initial offerings has been stolen." Pretty damning indictments, but how accurate are they in today's market, now that Bitcoin has achieved a fair degree of mainstream acceptance? It is undoubtedly true that Bitcoin's price is extremely volatile, but its volatility is due to a number of factors totally unconnected with the actions of potential fraudsters. It has been noticed by several observers that Bitcoin's price movements do follow the mainstream stock market indices, such as the Nasdaq and S&P. If these indices start to fall or rise, Bitcoin normally follows suit. Similarly, Bitcoin tends to rise when the dollar falls, and falls when the dollar rises. As Mansoor Mohi-uddin noted, liquidity has a significant effect on its volatility. In addition, over time investors have moved Bitcoin away from a solely retail base. Growing numbers of extremely savvy institutional investors, such as Tesla and MicroStrategy, have invested in Bitcoin, thereby fundamentally changing the Bitcoin investor base. These institutional investors have been shown to be storing their Bitcoins, not trading with them. These factors make it far more difficult for a single actor or even a small group of bad actors to manipulate the market. It should also be noted also that respected and prominent companies such Visa, PayPal, Mastercard and BNY Mellon have decided to support Bitcoin. This lends Bitcoin more credibility, as these companies would clearly not get involved in a scam which could destroy their reputations. Bitcoin may have a somewhat colourful past, but it now seems to have settled squarely in the mainstream financial system.

Finally, when you buy Bitcoin what do you get for your money? The short answer is a string of alphanumeric characters which represents your Bitcoin, and two codes which represent your private key (or secret key) and a public key. These keys show you are entitled to deal with the Bitcoin to which they relate. That doesn't appear much for $50–60,000, does it? However, an essential feature of Bitcoin is that it is a digital asset that you can send, resell or exchange for money. Holding Bitcoin gives you the ability to send your money anywhere in the world without using a bank and incurring bank fees. On top of this, there is always the possibility that your Bitcoin will appreciate in value.

So, what is Bitcoin? As we have seen, it is a digital asset which uses peer-to-peer technology to operate, with no central authority managing transactions. No one owns Bitcoin, and the issuing of Bitcoins is carried out collectively by the network. Bitcoin may have started life as an alternative to money generated by the centralised financial system, but over time it has developed into a much more flexible asset. Holders may use it as a currency, security or a commodity, depending on what they want to do with it.

Chapter 4

How does it work? – The digital nuts and bolts

Bitcoin was not the first attempt at a digital or decentralised currency. Some of the earlier examples were DigiCash, invented by David Chaum, B-Money created by Wei Dai, Bit Gold, founded by Nick Szabo and HashCash, introduced by Adam Beck. All these currencies failed to gain the necessary traction to succeed. They did, however, contribute to Bitcoin's success by providing elements that Nakamoto ultimately used in Bitcoin. For example,

- DigiCash introduced the concept of the combination of private and public keys to authenticate the identity of owners.
- B-Money used a decentralised network.
- Bit Gold provided the proof of work system, together with support for a decentralised system and the removal of the need for third party involvement.
- HashCash reinforced the use of a proof of work system to authenticate the validity of transactions.

One problem that all these coins failed to address was they did not deal with the issue of double payments. Nakamoto's introduction of blockchain solved this problem. In blockchain, timestamps are added at the end of previous timestamps based on a proof of work. Timestamps are used to create an unchangeable record of transactions.

Thus, in his 2008 paper Nakamoto introduced blockchain and Bitcoin. That paper showed how the Bitcoin network worked on blockchain. This has, unfortunately, led to some confusion. The term blockchain can sometimes refer to the original Bitcoin blockchain, and at other times to blockchain as a whole, encompassing other uses.

What is blockchain?

If Bitcoin needs the blockchain protocol to work, what is blockchain and how does it work for Bitcoin?

The basics of blockchain are pretty simple. A blockchain comprises a chain of blocks of information. This information is essentially a string of 0 and 1s. To protect these blocks of information, some people have permission to edit the information in the block and others only have authorisation to view it.

In practice, blockchain is primarily used by Bitcoin to record transactions. This record is also known as a distributed ledger or shared public ledger. Anyone can download it. In effect, this means the ability to download every transaction since 2009. There are also a number of sites where the public may view the ledger. Naturally, there are stringent measures in place to prevent anyone tampering with it.

How does blockchain work?

So when there is a transaction, who enters it in the ledger? No one owns Bitcoin, and there is no central body in charge of it. This means that the parties to the transaction must create a new block to be added to the chain. The new block contains information such as the amount of the transaction, its time, its date and the parties. The parties aren't actually named as such. Their identity is verified by their unique public and private keys, creating a digital signature. Before the block can be added to the chain, it must be verified. This is done by sending a message to other participants in the network, known as nodes. The verification process authenticates that the digital signature is valid and that the transaction's message is unspent. To prevent double spending, each block must have a unique code known as a hash. The hash is basically a cryptographic code created by algorithms. The cryptographic code is "solved" by a group of people known as "miners". These are the individuals who take on the responsibility for recording and verifying transactions. They are paid for this work in Bitcoin.

Once the code has been solved the answer is broadcast to the other nodes to be verified. Once verified, the block is added to the blockchain. The hash is used to link the new block to the previous block. In this way the chain's integrity is maintained. This approach also provides a security device. If someone seeks to alter a transaction, they must also alter all subsequent blocks. At this stage, the block can be viewed by everyone.

It can be readily seen that this verification process is vital to Bitcoin's credibility and integrity. The system itself is known as "proof of work". When Nakamoto published his Bitcoin white paper, he emphasised that proof of work was an essential feature of Bitcoin:

"We propose a solution to the double spending problem using a peer to peer network. The network timestamps transactions by hashing them into an ongoing chain of hash based proof of work, forming a record that cannot be changed without redoing the proof of work."

There are, of course, other advantages in the proof of work system:

- **It deters spammers and other malicious activity.** Due to the number of emails they would have to send out, a potential wrongdoer would not have the computational power to achieve their aim. In the event that they could come up with such computational power, the cost of sending out the enormous number of emails would be greater than any possible profits from doing so.
- **Security for the network.** The computational power required to overcome all the nodes working on the network and manipulate the system would be beyond the reach of a single player or even a group of players.

So let's take a look at the benefits and drawbacks of blockchain for Bitcoin.

Benefits

- Eliminates third party involvement.
- Reduces costs.
- Transactions are secure and private.
- Tampering with data is harder due to the proof of work security

system.
- More efficient, due to less human intervention.
- Transparency over the whole blockchain.

Drawbacks

- Mining costs.
- Low number of transactions processed per second.
- Scalability can be a problem, due to the consensus method.
- High energy consumption.

There is obviously a lot more to be said about the intricacies of blockchain and its workings. However, that is beyond the scope of this book and is a topic for another time.

Chapter 5

How do I buy Bitcoin? – The deal is done

Is it legal for me to buy Bitcoin?

You could be forgiven for thinking that buying a Bitcoin was a fairly simple process. For some people it is. For others, the options for buying Bitcoin may be restricted, and some may be banned from buying or holding Bitcoin at all.

So, at the beginning of a potential purchaser's journey to buy Bitcoin, they must first ensure that it is legal for them to do so. If it is legal, they must find out what conditions they will have to comply with.

Countries where it is illegal to buy, hold sell use or trade in Bitcoin

- Algeria
- Bangladesh
- Bolivia
- Cambodia
- China
- Colombia
- Ecuador
- Egypt
- Indonesia
- Iran
- Morocco
- Nepal
- Pakistan
- Saudi Arabia

- Taiwan

Countries which allow a limited use of Bitcoin

- India
- Jordan
- Nigeria
- Thailand
- United Arab Emirates
- Vietnam

In addition to this, countries have different regulations with regard to the types of investment vehicle you may use to hold Bitcoin. An example of this is Exchange Traded Funds (ETFs). Canada has authorised three Bitcoin ETFs. Australia is thinking about authorising ETFs with stringent consumer protection conditions. The US hasn't authorised any ETF to date, and the UK has banned them altogether. However, in all four countries it is perfectly legal to buy, hold, sell and use Bitcoins themselves.

So, a person's country of residence has a profound impact on whether they can buy Bitcoin and the form their Bitcoin investment may take.

Having established that it is OK to buy Bitcoin, what is the next step for the potential purchaser? First they will have to decide what form their purchase of Bitcoin will take. Will they be investing in a Bitcoin ETF or buying the coin itself?

What kind of Bitcoin investment do I want?

Before we go any further, let's look at what an ETF is. Basically, an ETF is an investment fund which tracks the price of an asset such as a commodity or a basket of shares. As the name suggests, ETFs are traded on exchanges in the same way as shares. This means that anyone can buy or sell their ETF on that exchange. ETFs tend to be cheaper than other funds, as they are passive index tracking funds. A Bitcoin ETF would obviously have Bitcoin as the underlying asset and would track the price of Bitcoin. The investor would not be buying the Bitcoin itself but would be acquiring it indirectly through the ETF portfolio. The major advantage of a Bitcoin ETF is that it makes Bitcoin easily accessible to a wide range of investors.

The other alternative is to purchase the Bitcoin itself. Many potential investors will look at Bitcoin's price of $50–60,000 and quite rightly say "I can't afford that". Well, there is good news about that. You don't have to buy a whole Bitcoin – you can buy fractions of it. Bitcoin is divided up into smaller units known as a Satoshi. One Satoshi equals 0.00000001 of a Bitcoin. It is therefore fairly easy to a buy a Satoshi or even part of one. Potential investors should also be encouraged by the fact that most new investors only spend $50–100 on their first cryptocurrency transaction.

So what is the difference between investing in a Bitcoin ETF and buying the coin itself? With an ETF, an investor acquires investment which is regulated by the authorities, and which they may buy and sell on an exchange. If an investor buys Bitcoin then there is little or no regulation, and they will have to make their own arrangements to store their Bitcoin. Storage of Bitcoin will be dealt with later in this chapter.

Investing in Bitcoin ETFs

It must be said that currently the range of choice of product in this type of investment is limited. There are three Bitcoin ETFs live on the Toronto exchange:

- Purpose Bitcoin ETF
- Evolve Bitcoin ETF
- CI Galaxy Bitcoin ETF

In addition to these three, the Brazilian Securities and Exchange Control Commission has given approval for the listing of the QR Capital ETF on the Sao Paulo B3 Stock Exchange. This ETF is composed entirely of Bitcoin and is due to go live in June 2021. They certainly seem popular. Purpose Bitcoin

ETF passed $1 billion in assets under management one month after its launch. There is now considerable pressure on regulators in both the US and Australia for the approval of proposed Bitcoin ETFs. This may lead to the choice of ETFs being substantially increased.

How to buy a Bitcoin ETF

If you are a Canadian or, from June 2021, a Brazilian, investing in Bitcoin ETFs is very easy. Citizens from other countries who wish to invest in the Canadian or Brazilian ETF will have to work a little harder. The first thing they need to do is find a broker or online trading platform with access to the Canadian or Brazilian stock exchanges. There are a number of global ETF brokers such as, amongst others, CMC, IG and etoro. The potential investor should compare the various brokers and platforms to see which best suits them, their circumstances and their investment aims. Once they have found a platform that suits them, they can get started on the road to investing.

- **Open your account.** The investor will need to complete an application to open an account on the platform. This is pretty straightforward, but sometimes questions are asked to determine the investor's knowledge of investing and the markets. The platform is required by the regulations to go through a process known as "know your customer". This entails the investor providing proof of their identity. This may take the form of pictures of a driving licence, passport, tax reference number, domestic bills and even a selfie. A note of caution is needed here. This part of the process can be either very easy or time-consuming and frustrating, depending on how well the software which uploads the pictures operates.

- **Fund your account.** Once the account is verified and opened, the investor will be invited to deposit funds into their account. Depending on the platform, this may be done by bank transfer, debit/credit card or PayPal. Another note of caution is needed. Some banks will block certain types of payment to some platforms. This may take the form of either a blanket ban, or a ban on, say, bank transfers while payments by a debit card are allowed. If their payment is blocked, the investor may have to find an alternative way to get money to and from their trading platform account.

- **Research and options**. The investor is almost ready to take the plunge. All they need to do now is to evaluate the market. How much do they want to buy? Do they want to buy at today's price? Or do they want to delay their purchase until the price suits their investment strategy? Once they have the answers to these questions, they can execute either a market order (immediate buy order) or a limit order (the buy is executed when the price reaches the level selected by the investor).

- **Watch the investment**. The ETF has now been bought, and all that remains is to keep track of it to ensure that it meets the investor's goals.

If the investor either does not want to own a Bitcoin ETF or is precluded from doing so, there are alternatives. Blockchain ETFs are available, which track companies with digital currency exposure, such as:

- Amplify Transformational Data Sharing ETF
- Reality Shares Nasdaq NexGen Economy ETF
- First Trust Indxx Innovative Transaction & Process ETF
- Capital Link Global Fintech Leaders ETF

How do I buy Bitcoin?

There are a number of ways to buy Bitcoins. For example:

- Brokers, such as Bitcoin.com's website.
- Peer to peer trading platforms.
- Cryptocurrency exchanges.

When embarking on any of these methods it is considered good practice first to set up a Bitcoin wallet. This is necessary, as the wallet is effectively the "address" where your Bitcoin will be sent, received and stored. The wallet may be used on any of your personal devices such as a phone, tablet, laptop or desktop. The wallet comes with a private and public key. The private key allows access to the Bitcoin, while the public key allows contact between one Bitcoin holder and another. It is of paramount importance to keep the private and public keys safe, as if they are lost there is precious little chance of recovering them and the Bitcoins will be lost.

OK. The potential investor needs a Bitcoin wallet, so where do they get it from? First, they need to find a wallet which suits their circumstances and needs. There are a number of very good wallets which can be downloaded such as:

- Exodus
- Wasabi
- Mycelium
- Electrum
- Trezor Model T

The investor will need to do their own research to find out which of these wallets, or indeed any of the others on the market, are suitable for them. Another alternative is to go to Bitcoin.com and download their wallet, which has a reputation for being secure and easy to use. Nearly 17 million Bitcoin.com wallets have been created so far.

The wallet has been selected and set up. Now the investor is ready to buy. All they need to do is decide what currency they are going to use and which method of purchase to adopt.

Typically, the procedures for using the various methods of buying Bitcoin are as follows:

Broker's website

- Visit the website.
- Select Bitcoin as the currency to be purchased.
- Enter the currency to be used for the purchase and the amount.
- Review the transaction details, add the wallet address and follow the on-screen instructions.
- Create an account and provide payment details to complete the transaction.

Peer-to-peer trading platform

- Review peer-to-peer trading platforms. Find one with good reviews which offers an escrow account to facilitate transactions. Create an account.
- Either find a seller who is trying to sell their Bitcoin or create a new buy order.
- Open a trade with the seller. The seller will send the Bitcoin to the escrow account.
- Send the agreed purchase price.
- Once the seller confirms receipt of the funds, the Bitcoin will be released from the escrow account and sent to the purchaser's wallet.

Cryptocurrency exchange

- Find a suitable cryptocurrency exchange.
- Create an account. The "know your customer" identity verification procedure outlined above will have to be completed.
- Follow the on-screen instructions to buy Bitcoin.
- The purchased Bitcoin will be transferred to the exchange wallet associated with the investor's exchange account.

- Move the Bitcoin from the exchange wallet to the investor's own wallet.

It is OK to leave Bitcoin in the exchange wallet. People do. However, the downside is that if someone hacks in and steals the Bitcoin it will probably be gone for good. This happened in the case of Mt. Gox, a Bitcoin exchange, which between 2013 and 2014 handled approximately 70% of Bitcoin transactions worldwide. In February 2014 it became clear that around 850,000 Bitcoins had disappeared from the company's cryptocurrency wallet. It is therefore thought to be more secure if the Bitcoin is held in the investor's own cryptocurrency wallet.

The Bitcoin has now been purchased. The next step is to make sure that it is secure. If the Bitcoin is safely tucked away in a wallet, what else needs to be done? The following steps are good practice and strongly recommended.

- **Create backups of private keys.** To prevent the loss of these vital components through theft, hard drive failure or other mishaps, the storing of a backup off-site is advised.

- **Never disclose private keys to anyone.** Never give anyone else details of your private keys unless you intend them to have access to your Bitcoin.

- **Software.** Make sure that the wallets are running on the latest version of the software, to ensure that they are as safe as possible.

Chapter 6

What can I do with my Bitcoin? Do I spend it or save it?

Now the Bitcoin has been bought, what can be done with it? Spend it? Spend it on what? Save it? Save it how, and what for?

Let's take spending first. There seems to be an assumption that people won't want to spend Bitcoins. Why not? Craig White, the professed creator of Bitcoin, says it was to meant to be a "successor to cash." However, there is a legion of stories about people spending their Bitcoin only to find out, with the subsequent movement of Bitcoin's value, that this was a very expensive purchase. Here are some examples:

- The first Bitcoin transaction, when Laszlo Hanyesz offered and paid 10,000 Bitcoins for two Papa John's pizzas. At the time 10,000 Bitcoins equalled about $50. Those 10,000 Bitcoins are now worth about $547,280,000. Very expensive pizza!

- The singer Lily Allen has said on Twitter that she was asked to stream a gig live on Second Life for hundreds of thousands of Bitcoin. She turned the offer down. Had she accepted, she would now be a billionaire.

- One Honda fan has posted on YouTube about how he spent 30.5 BTC (Bitcoins) on a used Honda NXS Targa and 6.5 BTC (Bitcoins) for another used Honda sports car. He says at the time he wasn't worried about paying in Bitcoin. Now, with 37 BTC equating to $2,022,457 he realises how much he has lost.

- Another Bitcoin investor transferred his Bitcoin onto a payment card and bought a meal deal from a UK supermarket for $4.87 or 0.0073 Bitcoin. At today's prices that means his sandwich cost him $288.85.

- Despite the potential for huge losses if people spend their Bitcoins, Bitcoins are still being spent on a regular basis. So, what kind of thing are people buying with their Bitcoin? The answer seems to be a wide variety of items. Here are some examples:

- The seller of a two-bedroom apartment in Brighton, UK, has said they will accept Bitcoin as payment.
- Core Bullion Traders in Ireland have announced that Bitcoin owners can now use their Bitcoins to buy gold on the Core Bullion Traders website.
- David Barral's transfer from Real Madrid B to Inter Madrid made history, as he is the first professional footballer whose transfer fee was paid entirely with Bitcoin.
- Tesla have announced that you can now buy your new Tesla car with Bitcoin.
- Bjork, the Icelandic pop star, has confirmed that she will accept Bitcoin in payment for her new album.

OK. So people are spending Bitcoin, and Bitcoin is being accepted as payment for goods and services. The next questions are, where do you go to spend Bitcoin and how do you find out who accepts it? There are over 100,000 outlets which accept Bitcoin. If the outlet accepts Bitcoin payments, they will generally indicate that they do so on their website or in their shop front window. Bitcoin.com and Coinmap both have excellent maps showing the locations and nature of outlets accepting Bitcoin.

Another important question is, what kind of outlets are they? Are they relevant to the people wanting to spend their Bitcoin? Here are some examples of where Bitcoin is accepted:

- **Local restaurants and shops.** A great many restaurants and shops have started to accept Bitcoin as payment. Thy indicate this on their websites or in their front windows. They take payments through either QR scanners or the Menufy app.
- **Shopify** hosts nearly 100,000 merchants on its platform and accepts Bitcoin as payment. Through Shopify you can gain access to an extremely wide variety of goods.

- **Bitpay.** A Bitpay card is accepted anywhere that accepts Visa. The Bitpay card is swiped like a normal debit or credit card.
- **Overstock** is another large platform where purchasers can pay for a diverse range of products using Bitcoin.
- **Travel.** You can use Bitcoin to pay for your vacation by booking through Expedia, CheapAir, Bitcoin.travel, TravelbyBit, CheapBizClass, Destinia, aBitSky, AirBaltic, Future.Travel and AirTreks.
- **Square.com.** A wide range of goods and services can be accessed through sellers who use Square.
- **Gambling.** You can gamble online using Bitcoin through Sportsbet, BetOnline, NitrogenSports, Betcoin and FortuneJack.
- **Microsoft** now accepts Bitcoin as payment for games and in-game purchases.
- **PC/Laptop.** Dell and Newegg accept Bitcoin as payment for certain PCs.
- **Gift Cards.** Home Depot, Sears and CVS accept payments in Bitcoin through the eGifter.com tool. QR scanners can be used for some in-store purchases.
- **Purse.io** helps you purchase goods on Amazon using Bitcoin.
- **Spendabit.** If you are looking for a product, Spendabit's search engine will tell you where you can buy it using Bitcoin.
- **Food.** Whole Foods, Starbucks, Baskin Robbins and Jamba Juice all accept Bitcoin payments.

The above list gives you a sense of just some of the market sectors where Bitcoin may be used. Bitcoin is also accepted by merchants in other sectors, such as PC and console games, clothing, accessories and hobbies. Some charities accept Bitcoin, so you can give to good causes. If you don't know what to buy someone for a present, you can always buy them a gift card with your Bitcoin.

It should also be remembered Mastercard, Visa and PayPal are now supporting Bitcoin payments to merchants using their platforms. When this is fully live, the list of places where you may spend your Bitcoin will increase by millions. Statista has calculated that Mastercard and Visa between them have 36 million locations accepting their cards. PayPal introduces over a million further merchants. Some merchants will accept at least two of the three, so there will obviously be some duplication. However, there will still be plenty of places to spend those Bitcoins.

There have also been some other interesting uses of Bitcoin:

- Russell Okung, a Carolina Panthers NFL football player, receives half of his $13 million salary in Bitcoin. It has been reported that players from the New York Yankees and Brooklyn Nets are also considering being paid this way.

- Miami is reported to be looking into using Bitcoin in a number of ways. This would include paying employees' salaries in Bitcoin, and allowing residents to pay their taxes in Bitcoin. Miami is also seeking permission from the State of Florida to invest city funds in Bitcoin. It is reported that other cities are thinking about this too.

- Dara Khosrowshahi, CEO of Uber, has said that the company would be open to accepting Bitcoin as payment.

As we have seen, you can use your Bitcoin to buy everything from an ice cream to a football player, and a myriad things in between.

We have some Bitcoin, and we don't want to spend it. We are going to save it. We are going to put it in our crypto wallet and leave it there. That raises a number of questions:

- We are not receiving any interest, so where is the benefit?
- What's the strategy behind doing this?
- Will the value of my Bitcoin be eroded by inflation?

Are we just going to sit back and hope that the price of our Bitcoin goes up? Is our strategy to hodl (which stands for "holding on for dear life")? Let's see what some of the big institutional investors are doing and why they are acting the way they are. MicroStrategy and Tesla have both invested part of their liquid cash into Bitcoin, $1.5 billion In Tesla's case. As the price of Bitcoin rose, they made more money from that investment than they did from selling their cars. However, perhaps the best explanation for companies taking this action comes from Lars Muller, the CEO of the German company SynBiotic. On February 16th, 2021, the company announced that it was moving part of its liquid cash into Bitcoin. The company's post on its website explained that the move was prompted by "legitimate concern about a massive devaluation of fiat money" caused by "excessive increase" in the Euro and US dollar supply. The company went on to say that "we have more long-term confidence in Bitcoin than in euros or dollars, where a central institution influenced by politicians can expand the money supply immeasurably."

This can be seen as the crux of the argument for adopting this approach. Bitcoin has a finite limit of 21 million. Accordingly, it has a scarcity value. It can't be expanded without the consensus of the holders, so its supply can't be increased to satisfy the exigencies of a particular country's economy or to facilitate the policy aspirations of particular politicians. This makes it an ideal hedge against the inflation and debasement of fiat currencies caused by the massive amount of money-printing by governments over the past decade or so. This move away from fiat currencies by major institutional investors is evidenced by the rapid increase in the number of owners who hold over 1,000 Bitcoin.

Apart from spending or saving our Bitcoin, what can we do with them? Obviously, we can wait for the price to rise, and sell at a profit. We could also exchange our Bitcoin for other cryptocurrencies, either because we feel they will do better or because they suit our investment criteria more closely. It is not difficult to complete either of these transactions. All that is required is that you follow these steps:

Cryptocurrency exchange

- Go to the exchange where you purchased your Bitcoin. Otherwise, open a new account with an alternative exchange. In this case you will have to verify your identity again.

- Follow the website's instructions for selling your Bitcoin.

- If you received fiat currency for your Bitcoin, you can either withdraw the cash to your bank account or purchase other cryptocurrency that is for sale in the exchange.

- If you swapped your Bitcoin for another cryptocurrency, transfer the coins to your personal crypto wallet.

Peer-to-peer trading platform

- Go to a suitable peer-to-peer trading platform. If you don't have an account, create one.

- Look for someone wishing to buy Bitcoin, or create a new sell order for yourself.

- Open the trade with the buyer and send your Bitcoin to the escrow account.

- Once you have received the purchase price, either in cash or in another cryptocurrency, confirm that you have been paid.

- Your Bitcoin will then be released from the escrow account and sent to the purchaser's wallet.

You can, of course, trade with your Bitcoin. There are numerous strategies for making money by taking advantage of rising and falling prices. This topic, however, is outside the scope of this book. Anyone looking to engage in this type of activity should seek help from a suitably-qualified financial adviser.

Chapter 7

Is Bitcoin safe? – Where did my Bitcoin go?

The safety of Bitcoin is a question that covers a huge area of concerns. It encompasses such questions as:

- Is Bitcoin a scam?
- Is Bitcoin a secure investment?
- Can Bitcoin be hacked?

Is it a scam?

What is a scam? The Cambridge English Dictionary defines a scam as "an illegal plan for making money, especially one that involves tricking people". Does Bitcoin meet this definition? First, as no one owns Bitcoin, who could be the bad actors hatching the illegal plan? There is no single driving force trying to trick investors out of their money. Second, as we have seen, Bitcoin has a number of functions depending on what the owner wishes to use it for. It can be used as a currency, an asset or a commodity. With its adoption by major institutional investors, bankers and credit/debit card companies, it has become mainstream. So, Bitcoin itself isn't a scam.

However, that doesn't mean that there are not lots of tricksters out there trying to scam Bitcoin investors. There are a number of scams set to trap the unwary investor, such as:

- **Bitcoin Profit.** Here the investor is gulled into believing they will receive high guaranteed returns which will make them rich, but they are really depositing their money with an unlicensed broker. The US District Court for the Southern District of New York recently fined Benjamin Reynolds, of Manchester, UK, $571 million for this type of scam. Reynolds told his customers he used advanced trading methods to generate guaranteed profits. He also offered to pay huge referral fees to customers to introduce their friends to his business. Through this scheme he received 22,190

Bitcoin from over 1,000 customers worldwide, which he misappropriated. At the time of the offence, the Bitcoin had a value of around $143 million. Perhaps the best advice here is, if it sounds too good to be true, then it probably is!

- **Social Media.** Using the power and visibility of social media, scammers have targeted Bitcoin owners. They have done this by hacking popular social media accounts or by creating bogus accounts themselves. Perhaps the most notorious example of this type of scam happened in 2020. The Twitter accounts of famous people such as Elon Musk and Bill Gates, and of companies such as Apple and Uber, were hacked. The hackers then posted tweets asking followers to send money to a specific address on the promise that the funds would be returned twofold as a charitable gesture. Apparently, there were several hundred takers within minutes of the posts going live. Once again, if it looks too good to be true, it probably is!

- **Social Engineering.** This scam happens when a scammer tries to gull you into disclosing personal information. This can include login details or passcodes. The fraudsters may contact their intended target through email, social media or by telephone. In the email approach (known as phishing) the email contains a fraudulent link. This is designed to obtain details of the Bitcoin owner's crypto wallet and the private keys required to gain access to the wallet and the funds it contains. Once they have this information, the scammers simply steal the Bitcoin in the wallet. To avoid this type of scam it is best not to click on the links in this sort of email. You can also check the email address to see if it contains the https syntax. Visiting unsecured websites is a really bad idea and can be very expensive.

- **Initial Coin Offering (ICO).** An ICO is cryptocurrency's version of an Initial Public Offering (IPO). Tricksters will, typically, create a bogus website that looks like an IPO. They will then scam investors into depositing their Bitcoins into a wallet controlled by themselves, so that they can misappropriate the coins.

- **DeFi "Rug Pulls".** This was the most popular scam of 2020. Its rise has come about as crypto investors look to increase their profits by entering yield-bearing investments. This scam involves persuading an investor to enter into a smart contract. This contract will require the investor to lock their coins in a fund for a specified period of time, in the expectation of a certain return. As soon as the contract expires, the developers use their program to steal the Bitcoin from the fund. An example of this type of scam is the theft from the DeFI platform Compounder Finance. The investors were promised compounded returns if they deposited their cryptocurrency into a smart contract which was time-locked. The developers created a backdoor into the fund and made off with a variety of cryptocurrencies worth around $750,000.

So, to avoid being scammed it is vital to conduct your own due diligence on any offering, and to remember above all the mantra that "if it sounds too good to be true, it probably is."

Is it a secure investment?

No one could deny that Bitcoin is a high-risk investment. It is after all a highly volatile unregulated investment. Some investors have seen massive profits on their investments as they have ridden market rises. Others have seen all or nearly all their investment disappear in market collapses.

US Treasury Secretary Janet Yellen has said of Bitcoin that "it is an extremely inefficient way of conducting transactions" and "It is a highly speculative asset and you know I think people should be aware it can be extremely volatile and I do worry about potential losses that investors can suffer." The Financial Conduct Authority in the UK has warned British consumers investing in digital assets they should be prepared to lose all their money.

Are they right? Yassine Elmandira, a cryptoanalyst at ARK, disagrees: "I really think that it's just outdated arguments as a function of their complete lack of education, which is a function of just their lack of interest in learning about this."

So, going forward, is Bitcoin to remain a volatile, speculative asset or will it become something more mainstream? As Danny Cox of Hargreaves Lansdown said, "Cryptocurrencies could remain niche, become mainstream, vanish without trace or anything in between." It is undoubtedly true that some cryptocurrencies will fail, and some that haven't even been thought of at the present time will in five or ten years' time be a major force in the market.

So, how does this apply to Bitcoin? Is it becoming mainstream? Signs that it may be can be found quite easily. Mark Hipperson CEO of ZIglu has said that "with more and more big brands such as Tesla and Starbucks accepting crypto there now seems to be little doubt that one day soon crypto will be accepted at as many places as traditional currencies." JP Morgan's analysts have been quoted as saying that there are "tentative signs" of diminishing volatility, which would encourage institutional investors in cryptocurrency. US regulators have also approved the listing of Coinbase, the largest digital currency exchange in the US. As we have seen, major banks and credit card companies are providing Bitcoin offerings to their customers. According to a report by Deutsche Bank, Bitcoin's market capitalisation of $1,089,407,069,181 makes it "too important to ignore."

A greater degree of stability will aid the progression of Bitcoin towards the mainstream. More large institutional investors will certainly help. Technical analysis seems to show that recent price movements aren't as extreme as in previous times. This may be a result of institutional investors activity squeezing some of the volatility out of Bitcoin's price movements.

However, as with any investment, it is essential to perform due diligence, and never to invest more than you can afford to lose. Blair Halliday, Head of UK at the Gemini cryptocurrency exchange, argued that chasing "very short term gains" could be risky, but that digital assets had a place as a long-term investment in a diversified portfolio.

Can it be hacked?

To answer this question, it is important to differentiate between the Bitcoin blockchain ecosystem itself and where the coins are stored after any transactions on the system.

The Bitcoin network is almost impossible to hack due to the nature of the technology underpinning it. Being decentralised, the data of the blockchain system used by Bitcoin is spread across multiple computers and is not stored on a central server. This means that if a hacker wants to get to any information, they must gain access to a huge number of computers, which makes their task a great deal harder. Since its launch in 2009, the entire Bitcoin network has not been hacked.

However, the picture with regard to exchanges and wallets isn't quite so rosy. The combined value of Bitcoin and other cryptocurrencies amounts to around a staggering $280 billion. Obviously, it is too tempting a target for hackers and bad actors generally to leave alone. Since its inception, attempts have been made to attack this asset pile, and there have been cases where exchanges and wallets have been hacked, such as the data breach at the French-based Bitcoin and cryptocurrency wallet Ledger. This involved the theft of personal information of over 270,000 Bitcoin and cryptocurrency users. This data was published on RaidForums, where hacked information is bought and sold.

If hackers can access details of the information required to access crypto wallets, they will steal Bitcoins. They may even do this by gaining access to the owner's non-Bitcoin related information. It is therefore essential to take the precautions set out in Chapter 5.

On the brighter side, it should be noted that the proceeds of cryptocurrency crime fell by over $5 billion in 2020. This was attributed largely to enhanced regulatory compliance by cryptocurrency exchanges and a falling number of scams. Hopefully, this is the start of a more secure environment for Bitcoin holders.

Chapter 8

Bitcoin Pros and Cons

We have now taken a look at where Bitcoin came from, what it is, how it works and what you can do with it. In its early days Bitcoin received a very bad press. It was seen as tool for criminals to launder the proceeds of crime and for terrorists to fund their activities. It was also seen as a scam, due to the activities of bad actors who lured novice investors with fraudulent promises of massive profits and/or used fake celebrity endorsements to promote their products.

As we have seen, some consider Bitcoin to be a currency of the future. However, Bitcoin can also be used by the holder as an asset or a commodity. When Bitcoin is utilised this way, the holder is using it purely for its speculative and volatile nature.

The extraordinary rise in the price of Bitcoin has led to intense media and investor interest. This in turn has gained Bitcoin increased popularity. As we have seen, many payment platforms such as Mastercard, Visa and PayPal have started to accept payments in Bitcoin. It is becoming easier to trade Bitcoins on established platforms.

As the understanding of Bitcoin and its underlying technology grows, it is being seen in a more positive light. Now is therefore the time to look at its benefits and disadvantages, in order to make an informed judgement on Bitcoin's viability and potential for success.

Benefits of Bitcoin

Identity

- You are not required to supply personal information when making a Bitcoin payment.
- The only information that is viewable is your public key (public address). The personal information relating to it cannot be seen.
- Bitcoin transactions are private and anonymous.

Security

- Bitcoin transactions are irreversible, which protects merchants against fraud and fraudulent chargebacks. This is clearly an incentive for traders to adopt it.
- No personal information is displayed, which makes the transaction safe from identity theft.
- Bitcoin's system is safe due to the fact that it is cryptographically secured, and so cannot be tampered with.
- Trade can continue even in areas known for high crime and fraud rates, because Bitcoin's public register makes it very difficult to mislead anyone.

Control

- Bitcoin provides complete payment freedom. It can be transferred to anyone, anywhere in the world 24/7, 365 days of the year. Such transfers are not subject to the usual limitations such as holidays, payment limits or strikes. This is a massive advantage.
- There is no one person or entity in control of Bitcoin, so the owner is in complete control of their money.
- It is not possible for traders to add extra fees without the prior consent of the Bitcoin owner.

Transparency

- Every completed transaction is visible to everyone.

Fees and charges

- Bitcoin payments attract very low fees or none at all.
- It is possible to include fees to have a transaction processed faster.
- Traders can use digital currency exchanges to convert Bitcoins into fiat money (government-backed currency). The fees to do this

are generally lower than those charged by credit card companies or PayPal.

Non-inflationary

- Excessive governmental money-printing causes fear of debasement of the currency and an increased risk of inflation. Since the financial crisis of 2008/2009, the Federal Reserve's balance sheet has increased eightfold, the European Central Bank's approximately fourfold, and the Bank of Japan's around sevenfold.
- Money-printing is not possible with Bitcoin. There can only ever be 21 billion Bitcoins and approximately 18.7 billion are already in existence.

Growing acceptance and usage

- Institutional investor interest in buying and holding Bitcoin is increasing.
- Payment platforms such as Mastercard, Visa and PayPal are allowing Bitcoin to be used for transactions by their customers.
- There has been a huge growth in the number and diversity of outlets accepting payments in Bitcoin.
- Mainstream banks are providing Bitcoin offerings to their customers.

Possibility of high returns

- The price of one Bitcoin quadrupled over the course of 2020.

Disadvantages of Bitcoin

Volatility and possibility of large losses

- Bitcoin's price can be subject to quite dramatic fluctuations. However, analysis of the charts shows that these movements are not as extreme as in previous years.

- There is a degree of volatility to Bitcoin due to liquidity issues. Basically, there are a limited number of Bitcoins available and a strong demand for them. This will be mitigated, and Bitcoin will become more stable over time with greater market capitalisation and as more businesses accept it as a means of payment.
- The timing of any investment in Bitcoin can have a major impact on the returns gained.

Degree of acceptance

- Many people still don't know what Bitcoin is or how to use it.
- Although more and more businesses are accepting Bitcoin, the number needs to grow dramatically for its full network effect to be felt.
- Workers need to be educated about Bitcoin, otherwise companies will advertise their acceptance of Bitcoin, but their staff will not know what it is or how to process it.

No safety net

- Due to Bitcoin's decentralised nature, no one is in control of it. If you lose your Bitcoins there isn't a body or organisation can retrieve or replace them for you. Bitcoin is not like a credit or debit card. There isn't a company you can contact to request a replacement.
- If you lose the details to gain access to your Bitcoin wallet, you have lost all the Bitcoins in that wallet. This is no one you can contact to request a password reset. This is why it is vital to back up your wallet access information.

Development stage

- Bitcoin is still in its early stages, and many of the features which will make it safer and more accessible are still being developed and tested.

- There may be teething problems which will need ironing out.
- Bitcoin has some way to go to reach its full potential.

Conclusion

Bitcoin is neither a finished article nor perfect. It does have certain advantages which are beneficial to users. On the other hand, it also has some disadvantages which can impact on potential investors. There is the potential to make large profits but also to incur large losses. Awareness is still a potential issue. Some of Bitcoin's disadvantages may be put down to the fact it is still in the process of development. However, Bitcoin does have some advantages not shared by other forms of currency. Not least of these is having the blockchain system at its core, which has the potential to reduce costs and make the financial system more efficient.

In the final analysis it is up to the individual to balance the pros and cons before making a decision on what way, if any, they are going to use Bitcoin.

www.ingramcontent.com/pod-product-compliance
Lightning Source LLC
LaVergne TN
LVHW081545060526
838200LV00048B/2222